The Spirit of the PERFORMANCE HORSE

The photographs in this book celebrate the people and horses involved with American performance horse sports at the highest levels of excellence. Robert Dawson, America's most gifted horse photographer, has captured the enchanting world of performance horses and equestrian athletes in 128 outstanding images. The text includes brief histories and descriptions of Dressage, Show Jumping, Three-day Event, Four-in-Hand Driving and Carriage Driving. It includes, as well, personal profiles of renowned individuals in each discipline whose skill and knowledge have allowed them to make outstanding contributions to the sport. Many fine books have chronicled the illustrious history of the United States Equestrian Team in competition, both in photographs and in text. This book captures the essence of this special equestrian community at home; both at national horse shows and at the picturesque farms coast to coast that are homes to America's most celebrated performance horses.

PHOTOGRAPHY BY ROBERT DAWSON
TEXT AND EDITING BY TAMMY LEROY · FOREWORD BY JENNIFER O'NEILL

Copyright ©2003 PRIMEDIA Enthusiast Publications, Inc.
d/b/a PRIMEDIA Equine Network

All rights reserved. No part of this book may be reproduced or transmitted in any form or by any means, electronic or mechanical, including photocopying, recording, or by any information storage or retrieval systems, without the written permission of the publisher.

Photography - Robert Dawson , www.dawsonphotography.com

Text & Editing - Tammy LeRoy

Design and Production – Bryan E. Daws, Dawsign Communications Design Studio
www.dawsign.com

Front Cover Design – Ketch Design

Publisher by PRIMEDIA Enthusiast Publications, Inc.
d/b/a PRIMEDIA Equine Network
PRIMEDIA Equine Network
656 Quince Orchard Road, Suite 600
Gaithersburg, MD 20878
301.977.3900

VP, Group Publishing Director: Susan Harding
Director of Product Marketing: Julie Beaulieu

To Order call 800.952.5813
Order online at TheEquineCollection.com

Also available from The Equine Collection:
Along the Cowboy Trail and *The Spirit of the Horse,* by RD Publishing Inc.

Printed in Korea

ISBN 1-929164-17-3

Dawson, Robert, 1952-
  The spirit of the performance horse / photgraphy by Robert Dawson ;
text and editing by Tammy LeRoy ; foreword by Jennifer O'Neill.
     p. cm.
  ISBN 1-929164-17-3 (hardcover)
  1. Competition horses. 2. Competition horses--Pictorial works. I.
LeRoy, Tammy. II. Title.
  SF294.3 .D27 2003
  636.1'0022'2--dc21
                        2003001598

FOREWORD

Although my childhood connection with horses was dismissed by my parents as the passing fancy of every little girl, it, in fact, turned into a lifelong love story that has remained my faithful affair of the heart for the past forty-five years. To date, I have bred over one hundred horses, shown on the "A" circuit for over thirty-five years, won in the best company, and paid my dues as an owner, breeder, rider and farm manager. Most importantly, I never gave up on my childhood dream.

In my autobiography, *Surviving Myself*, I open with the following passage: "There is a laughter so deep within us that it cannot be contained. There is a singing that comes from our very souls. There are record-breaking Olympic moments, births, springtimes, and lovemaking. . . . And sometimes there is a unique ballet that happens between animal and man; a melding of muscle, mind, and spirit that identifies two as one. That's what it feels like to jump a fence in perfect harmony with your horse. That's why I love the sport so much. . . . It requires a marriage between an animal that weighs at least ten times more than you, has moods, physical limitations, and a mind to win or not. Mutual rhythm, respect, and heart make a special horse-and-rider team, and if you've ever known that, even for a moment, you can't help but want more."[1]

It is one thing to attempt to express the profound and penetrating impact horses have on so many of us with the written word, but, as it is said, "a picture is worth a thousand words." Fortunately, Robert Dawson is an absolute master with the lens. His freeze-framed photographs of horses are nothing less than inspirational. What is truly unique about Robert's style, beyond its stunning composition and use of color, is his choreography of the moment. He stages each scene the way film directors reveal a movie's theme, presenting the story as if the audience just happened to pass by during a dramatic pause. Robert's work stirs my very soul.

From one horse lover and film maker to another . . . bravo and bravo!!

— God Bless
Jennifer O'Neill

[1] Excerpt from *Surviving Myself*, by Jennifer O'Neill, William Morrow & Company (1999)

PREFACE

The photographs in this book celebrate the people and horses involved with American performance horse sports at the highest levels of excellence. Robert Dawson, our nation's most gifted horse photographer, has captured the enchanting world of horses and riders in 128 outstanding images. The text includes brief histories and descriptions of Dressage, Show Jumping, Three-day Event, Four-in-hand Driving and Carriage Driving. It includes, as well, personal profiles of renowned individuals in each discipline whose skill and knowledge have allowed them to make outstanding contributions to the sport. Many fine books have chronicled the outstanding history of the United States Equestrian Team, both in photographs and in text. This book captures the essence of this special equestrian community at home; both at national horse shows and at the picturesque farms coast to coast that are homes to America's most celebrated performance horses.

While compiling this collection many individuals afforded our project their unfailing support and enthusiasm. They did so because of their passionate dedication to performance horse sports. Their unselfish contributions of their time were the propelling force that drove the project forward. As outsiders to this unique equestrian world, we looked to its participants to choose individuals whose contributions to each discipline they deemed most valuable. Again and again, the names of particular men and women resurfaced. Portions of this book are dedicated to profiles of these special few: Debbie McDonald, a Pan-American Gold Medallist in Dressage; George Morris, an Olympic and Pan-American individual medallist who has served as Chef d'Equipe of several U.S. Olympic Show Jumping teams; Captain Mark Phillips, one of the world's leading Three-day Event riders who, as Chef d'Equipe of the USET Eventing squad, has helped the team bring home Gold and Bronze medals; Hardy Zantke, Chef d'Equipe of the U.S. Four-in-Hand Driving team that took the Silver Medal at the 2002 World Equestrian Games; and Gloria Austin, whose expertise and devotion to the gracious art of Carriage Driving is unrivaled in our country. Not only did these distinguished individuals agree to include their personal experiences and wisdom in this book, they also were willing to explain patiently the fundamentals and nuances of their particular disciplines to uninformed newcomers.

This book project began with Ashley Dorrance, a lover of performance horses who is a neighbor of Robert Dawson. She and Ceinwen Rhys-Evans soon introduced Robert to Anke Magnussen, without whom this book could not have emerged. Through Anke's belief in the project, her knowledge of the horse world, and her invaluable help, we were introduced to many of the nation's top equestrian athletes and trainers. Soon Robert was invited to photograph many of the country's top horses at some of the most spectacular farms in the U.S. To Will and Nicki Simpson, Mary Tyng, Peter Fletcher, Heidi Austin-Fish, Suzanne Tucciarone, Misty Cassar, David and Karen O'Connor, Sandy Phillips, Bob McDonald, Cameron Fitch and Jami Jensen, we remain indebted, not only for their collective expertise, but also for the warm manner in which they welcomed us as newcomers.

Much of the research necessary for this book was made available by Janice Halpern and Marty Bauman from the public relations staff of the United States Equestrian Team. We owe a great debt as well to Jennifer O'Neill, who graciously agreed to write a foreword to this book. Though she has been known worldwide as a model, film star and author, we have come to admire her as a devoted horsewoman and as a warm and generous human being. Finally, the keen eye and constant support of Priscilla Aydelott made both the text and the challenging days before publication flow much more smoothly.

At the project's beginning we awkwardly navigated through a previously unfamiliar world. Within a year we had become permanent fans of performance horse sports, and we spent a nail-biting week in September scanning the news wires as the USET made history in Spain at the 2002 World Equestrian Games. It was by far the best U.S. performance at any World Equestrian Games. American riders, drivers and vaulters won a total of eight medals, doubling the nation's best previous performance. We would like to take advantage of this opportunity to express our pride and gratitude to the USET athletes and the people behind the scenes who often go uncelebrated: the chefs d'equipe, trainers, handlers, veterinarians and sponsors who help carry them to victory.

The world of performance horses is one of colorful drama and breathtaking excitement as well as one of pastoral vistas and quiet communion between man and horse. Robert Dawson has captured these moments on film as only he can. It is our hope and our goal that this book will serve as a reminder of why humans always have revered the majestic horse, and why equestrian sports have thrilled mankind for thousands of years.

— Tammy LeRoy
Author/Editor

INTRODUCTION

AMERICA'S LEGACY IN PERFORMANCE HORSE SPORTS

Equestrian excellence has been valued in the Americas since the Spanish first brought horses to the West Indies in 1493. In 1519, Spanish soldiers headed by Hernando Cortez introduced horses to Central America. The advantages of the mounted warrior played a pivotal role in the ability of the European invaders to conquer the Native peoples who populated a land that had long been inhabited; one which the newcomers dubbed the New World. Native Americans, who were quick to adopt new technologies, soon incorporated domesticated horses into their cultures, and many became expert horsemen. During the later era of Spanish reign over the western region of what is now the United States, the Californios developed an economy centered on cattle ranching, and in the later 1700s, vaqueros of Indian and Spanish ancestry became the forerunners of the American cowboy.

On America's eastern shores, Germans, Swedes, and other Europeans who settled brought horses as well. Europeans as well as Asians and Middle Easterners had been developing the art of horsemanship for at least four millennia, and colonists imported their knowledge, skills, and breeding stock to the New World. In the late 1600s, most New England families owned at least one horse. Towns were erected eight to ten miles apart, a distance covered by a horse in about an hour. Horses were used primarily as transportation, draft animals, and cavalry mounts, but equine sporting in America began soon after colonization. Hunting on horseback helped provide food, but it was more often a form of diversion that broke the monotony of daily life. Hares, raccoons and opossums were hunted on horseback with dogs, much like fox hunting in England, although hunting these animals in this manner was less practical than catching them by trapping or other means. Early Americans also had a passion also for horse racing, but only the wealthy class could afford to breed horses solely for sport. The first known American turf race was held in New York in 1665.

Even among the poorer classes, however, horsemanship was a necessary skill in Early America. Until the twentieth century, most advanced training in equitation was limited to men serving in the military. Horse shows were originated by Ireland's Royal Dublin Society in 1864, and in 1868, the show included jumping competitions for the first time. The National Horse Show, America's oldest indoor show, was founded in 1883 at the original Madison Square Garden. Notable competitors included generals John J. "Black Jack" Pershing, William Billy Mitchell, and George S. Patton. One of the most successful competitive riding styles was taught at the U.S. Army Mounted Services School at Ft. Riley, Kansas. It was based on the styles of the *Ecole de Cavalerie* in France and the Italian Cavalry School.

The idea of including equestrian sports in the Olympics was raised when the first Olympic Games were being planned for 1896 in Athens, however, the idea did not gain enough support. An equestrian program prepared by Count Rosen of Sweden was introduced for the first time at the 1912 Olympic Games in Stockholm. Sixty-two competitors representing ten nations participated in the competitions. The Eventing competition was limited to military officers, but the Jumping and Dressage were open to civilians. The U.S. Army assumed the responsibility for preparing an equestrian team for the 1912 Olympic games. Military personnel may have been the only U.S. equestrians formally trained in European equestrian tradition at the time. Through the 1948 Olympics, the U.S. Army Equestrian Team served as the U.S. Olympic team as well, representing the country in all the games until 1952.

Captain Guy V. Henry, Jr. was named team leader of the five officers and eighteen horses that would make up the U.S. Equestrian Team. The small group that began training at Fort Riley, Kansas, in the chilly winter temperatures of early 1912, launched a legacy of equestrian excellence in America. They trained resolutely through early summer of 1912, and in June the team sailed with the other U.S. competitors bound for the Olympic games. They had resolved that the Three-day Event would be the focus of their efforts. When they arrived in Sweden the team drilled relentlessly, always striving to meet Captain Henry's uncompromising standards. During the event the U.S. Eventing team challenged for the Silver Medal unsuccessfully but amazed the Europeans by winning the Bronze. From then on, the U.S. was recognized as an impressive equestrian power.

It became clear after the 1912 Olympics that internationally recognized rules for the three disciplines were necessary. In 1921, representatives from ten countries met in Lausanne to discuss the formation of an international federation, and the *Fédération Equestre Internationale* (FEI) was born.

Nationally, too, there was a need for conformity in horse shows. In 1917 representatives of fifty American horse shows met in New York City to form a national organization dedicated to establishing fair competition in the show ring. The first annual meeting of the Association of American Horse Shows was held in 1918. Twenty-six well-known shows, including Brooklyn, Bryn Mawr, Devon, Tuxedo and Wilmington, were elected to membership. In 1935, the responsibility for U.S. membership in the FEI was granted to the American Horse Show Association. Today, USA Equestrian, the name adopted by the AHSA in 2001, recognizes 26 breeds and disciplines, has over 80,000 individual members, and sponsors more than 2,700 competitions at all levels.

The United States Equestrian Team is an organization that selects, trains, equips and finances equestrians to represent the U.S. in major international competition, including the Olympics Games and the World Championships.

The organization supports six disciplines: Dressage, Show Jumping, Three-day Event, Combined Driving, Endurance, and Reining (USET's first western riding discipline). The USET seeks out and fosters the development of talented equestrian athletes. Athletes representing the USET have achieved outstanding success over the last four decades, many times with the help and expertise of European-born trainers who have devoted their time to the development of the American team. The U.S. has gained elite status as an equestrian power by winning world championships in Show Jumping, Eventing, Endurance and Combined Driving. An impressive record of 27 Olympic and 61 Pan American Games Medals make American equestrians formidable challengers at the international level.

In 1990, the FEI brought six important world championships together at a single venue for the first time. The first World Equestrian Games were held in Stockholm, and featured Show Jumping, Dressage, Vaulting, Endurance, Three-day Event and Driving. At the 2002 World Equestrian Games in Jerez de la Frontera, Spain, the U. S. Equestrian Team doubled the nation's previous wins, bringing home a total of eight medals. U.S. teams won World Championship medals in six of the seven disciplines with three Gold, three Silver and two Bronze medals.

America's legacy in performance horse sports, though young when compared to the European tradition, is one in which the nation can take great pride. In less than a century, U.S. equestrians have achieved a remarkable record of success in international competition. The twenty-first century undoubtedly holds the promise of even greater accomplishments for the extraordinary group of American athletes – both human and equine – that rival the world's greatest.

The Art of Dressage

The art of dressage is a graceful and beautiful display of skillful collaboration between horse and rider. Developed more than two thousand years ago, the object of dressage is the development of the athletic ability of the horse in a harmonious blending of its physical characteristics and its natural temperament. It is not only a competitive sport but is also the training method considered fundamental to all performance horse sports. Although domesticated horses have been used for transportation for at least four thousand years, most evidence indicates that for the first two thousand years of domestication, little about the nature of the horse was understood or considered.

Artifacts dating back three thousand years suggest that horsemen in Mesopotamia used brutal training techniques, such as spiked bits, to control horses. The ancient Greeks are credited with creating the more enlightened method we now call Dressage – a French word for "training." The Greek civilization valued logic, balance, and the laws of nature, and found beauty in symmetry, which was applied to the art of horsemanship. Xenophon, a Greek military commander who was

Betsy Steiner on Rainier

born about 430 BC, wrote the earliest known training manual on horsemanship. Much of what he wrote in the work titled *Hippike* is still accepted by equestrian trainers today.

The Greeks used hot-blooded, purebred stallions as battle horses, believing they were the bravest and had the best athletic ability. The courage of these battle steeds has often been overlooked in the annals of history, as has the bravery of all war-horses throughout the centuries. Even the most skilled cavalryman was unlikely to be successful if mounted on a timid horse. Xenophon's battle experience allowed him to observe the various riding styles of many cultures with which the Greeks were at war. He developed a style in which consideration of both the horse's physique and psyche was fundamental. "Anything forced or misunderstood," he wrote, "can never be beautiful."

Although the Greek's training methods were designed primarily to give mounted soldiers the greatest advantage in battle, it was the importance placed on aesthetics that allowed the ancient civilization to develop horsemanship into an art form. For a well-trained dressage horse, difficult but natural movements such as leaps, turns, and pirouettes are executed with such precision and grace that they appear effortless.

When the Romans conquered Greece in 146 BC, they embraced much of Greek culture, including classical dressage. The fall of Rome in 410 AD marked the onset of the Middle Ages. Light and agile horses gave way to heavy, cold-blooded breeds, and the Greek and Roman cavalrymen schooled in classic horsemanship were replaced with armor-clad knights who relied on brute

Morning at Los Cedros Farms, Arizona

force rather than maneuverability. The advent of firearms in the Renaissance period revived the popularity of swift, agile breeds such as

the Spanish Barb and the Lusitanian. Today, the breeds favored in most performance horse sports are those that have been crossbred to produce lively but powerful warm-bloods. After Spanish horses were introduced to Italy circa 1500, the upright, balanced-seat "gineta" style became the mode, and it is practiced still in competitive dressage.

The equitation style of the court of Louis XIV was known as the School of Versailles. Francois Robichon de la Gueriniere (1688-1751) was one of the great masters of the era. His book, *L'Ecole de Cavalerie*, published in 1729, formed the foundation for training at the renowned Spanish Riding School of Vienna. Again, working in harmony with a horse's natural abilities and

inclinations were fundamental elements of the training style. "The knowledge of the nature of a horse is one of the first foundations of the art of riding it," de Gueriniere wrote, "and every horseman must make it his principal study."

The classic riding style of the Ecole de Cavalerie also was taught to military officers in the United States. Horsemanship was one of the few subjects at West Point Military Academy in which Ulysses S. Grant excelled, and Robert E. Lee's father was the famous general, Henry "Light-Horse Harry" Lee, a renowned cavalry officer who was one of George Washington's most trusted aides during the Revolutionary War. In the mid-nineteenth century, the U.S. Army Mounted Services School at Ft. Riley, Kansas, became America's premier equestrian training grounds. General George S. Patton, Jr., graduated from the Advanced Cavalry School at Ft. Riley.

Until the twentieth century, the study of classical horsemanship was reserved for the military and for affluent members of society. In 1912, competitive Dressage split from classical riding when it became part of the Stockholm Olympic Games. Although most of the early Olympic equestrians were cavalrymen, Olympic sport status meant that competitive Dressage was open to a broader range of citizens.

~17

Competitive Dressage

The refined images of competitive Dressage reflect equestrian methods that have been practiced for centuries in all advanced civilizations. Today, its grand traditions are carried on in the show ring where gleaming, meticulously-groomed horses carry riders elegantly turned out in white breeches, black tail coats, yellow waist-coats, black boots, white stock ties, white gloves and black top hats. This attention to detail starts with good horsemanship. Quality veterinary care, proper feeding, and an ongoing training program are the foundations in Dressage. Correctly fitted equipment and good grooming are also necessary. The general, overall appearance of horse and rider is much more important in Dressage than in other equestrian disciplines. Dressage is a performance, and, as such, competitors strive to look as beautiful as nature will allow. Both should be turned out immaculately, with everything gleaming and in place. This makes it easy for a judge to give the benefit of the doubt to the combination that pleases the eye.

Dressage horses can be of any breed, sex, age, color or size. In a potential Dressage horse, riders look for exceptional basic paces – walk, trot and canter, together with a good temperament and sound conformation.

The horse should have athletic paces, should be light on its feet, and should have the scope of ability to take short, springy strides as well as free, long and swinging ones.

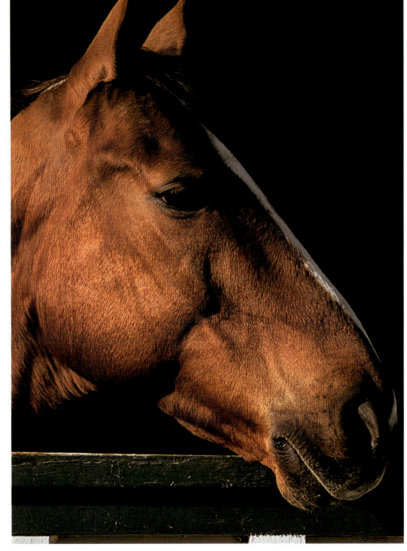

When Dressage is practiced as a sport, competitors pursue the unobtainable 100 percent. Meticulous attention to detail is necessary in addition to ability. Marks may be out of reach because of a lack of talent, experience or technique, but they should not be thrown away for lack of preparation.

Competitive Dressage takes place in a 20x60-meter arena, with twelve lettered markers placed at specific points along the rail. Here, horse and rider perform a designated test that is a series of movements for which the arena markers serve as reference points. The origin of the peculiar sequence of the letters is unknown.

Different levels of tests are offered in international Dressage competition.

Steffen Peters on Grandeur

In order of difficulty, they are Young Rider Tests, Prix St. Georges, Intermediaire I, Intermediaire II, and Grand Prix. Within the Grand Prix level are the Grand Prix, the Grand Prix Special and the Grand Prix Freestyle – a performance the rider choreographs to music. In the Freestyle, particular movements must be performed, and each performance has a time limit. Outside of these limitations, the competitor can create any program that suits his or her horse, and is especially pleasing to the eye.

The most spectacular movements within the horse's natural range of abilities can be seen during the international tests: Piaffe, the highly collected, elevated trot in place; Passage, the suspended trot in slow-motion; Pirouette, a rhythmic turning in place at the walk and canter; Half Pass, a forward and sideways movement at the

Guenter Seidel on Nikolaus 7

trot or canter in which the horse crosses his legs; and the Flying Change, a skipping type movement at the canter in which the horse changes lead every fourth, third, second, and finally, at every stride. None of these movements are tricks – all are natural and are performed by horse's at play. With careful training, the horse learns to duplicate these natural movements willingly, on command, and with grace while accommodating the weight of a rider. The trust and harmony that makes this possible are a tribute to the rider's ability and to the horse's generosity.

One to five judges evaluate each individual's performance. Scores range from zero (not executed) to 10 (excellent), with each movement receiving a "mark." Particular movements in each test are emphasized more than others, so marks for these moves are multiplied by factors of 2, 4 or 6. The judges are also required to award "collective marks" for paces, impulsion and submission of the horse, and also for the position of the rider. These scores usually relate to the overall impression of the test as a whole. The scoring standard is absolute perfection, and competition scores at the Olympic level, which is the sport's highest, normally fall in the 70 percent range.

USET Dressage Arena at Gladstone, New Jersey

The way the horse moves on straight and curved lines is important. On the straight, its body should be straight with the hind feet following the same path as the fore feet. On turns and circles, the horse's body should bend uniformly along the arc in order to create the same path with fore and hind feet. Circles should be round and smooth, and turns should be even. Transitions between

~25

gaits should also be smooth, and the horse should immediately establish a rhythm in the new gait. When the horse extends or collects its gaits, there should be an obvious difference in the length of its stride. During an extension the horse's frame is lengthened, and each stride should increasingly cover more ground. During a collected movement the frame is shortened, and each stride should cover less ground without any loss of impulsion or energy. The horse should carry its head in a vertical position, indicating acceptance of the bit, and continually feeling for the rider's aids. The horse travelling with its nose either stiffly held out in front or overly bent toward its chest is not accepting the rider's hand.

The rider should maneuver the horse through the test without apparent effort, maintaining balance, with the upper body erect but supple. Thighs and legs should be steady and stretched downward. The elbows should be held close to the body, giving the rider the ability to follow the horse's movements and to apply the aids imperceptibly. When performed well, the combination of athletic ability, physical grace, and visual pleasure makes Dressage a wonderful sport for participants and spectators alike. The blending of discipline, demanding work and artistry, in a harmonious partnership between horse and rider, is the greatest appeal of Dressage.[1]

[1] Description provided by the United States Equestrian Team, 2002.

Betsy Steiner on Rainier floating through the USET Dressage selection trials for the 2002 World Equestrian Games

Debbie McDonald
A World-Class Champion

Debbie McDonald in competition on Bretina

At the 2002 World Equestrian Games, Debbie McDonald, riding a beautiful chestnut Hanoverian mare named Brentina, made history by bringing home a Bronze Medal in individual freestyle competition. It was the best performance offered by an American combination of horse and rider in World Games history. "She may have taken the bronze, but her personality deserves a Gold," says Steffen Peters, who won a team Bronze medal in Dressage at the 1996 Olympic games. McDonald has trained with Steffen, and he calls himself her biggest fan. Steffen attributes McDonald's success to excellent discipline, dedication, intelligence, an eye for good horses, and sensitivity in working with them.

Debbie McDonald was born in Pomona, California, and grew up in the Costa Mesa-Newport Beach area. Her love of horses began when, as a child, she travelled to Kansas each summer to visit an uncle who always had a horse for her to ride. "Something inside of me was aching to have a horse of my own," McDonald remembers. "But my father was in bad health, and my family couldn't afford a horse." One day, she saw a pony

Debbie McDonald at home on River Grove Farms

Debbie's first day at the USET Dressage Trials

advertised in the newspaper for $500. Both she and her father fell in love with the pony when they went to see it. "Somehow," she says, "my dad found the money to buy it, with the stipulation that I had to help with the cost of keeping it."

McDonald was able to keep the pony at the Orange County Fairgrounds where she worked in trade for its board. The only available stall was near a man who kept gaited horses. One day, she showed up at the stables to find him whipping her pony. His explanation was that it wasn't "animated" enough. McDonald took the pony and wandered the grounds crying, as she searched for an empty stall. She ended up at Bob McDonald's barn, and she told him the story. Bob offered to stable her pony at his barn, and Debbie cleaned stalls for him after school. Bob, who was involved with hunter-jumpers, sometimes gave her riding lessons.

Debbie McDonald giving instruction at home

She also grew fond of his daughter, Kim. Eventually she outgrew the pony and bought a horse. She became a competent rider although she could not afford to show.

When Debbie was fifteen, she met Perry and Peggy Thomas and their daughter Jane, who was nine. Peggy Thomas liked Bob's manner with kids. He was strict, but never used bad or insulting language. Peggy stayed to watch every lesson Jane took with Bob. Eventually, the Thomas family bought Jane a great thoroughbred named Beau Valentine. When Debbie was eighteen, Jane was entered to compete in a show at the fairgrounds. When the day of the show arrived, Jane couldn't attend, and Debbie showed Beau Valentine in her stead. "It was my first break," she recalls. "We won almost every class." The Thomases bought other horses with Bob, which Debbie rode and showed while Jane was away at school.

By the time Debbie was twenty, her friendship with Bob had developed into a romance. The two have been together for twenty-five years. Their son, Ryan, was born in 1983. In 1982 they moved to Sun Valley, Idaho, when Peggy Thomas asked Bob to relocate there so she could have her horses near her home. Together, they designed a wonderful horse facility. After the move Peggy became interested in showing Beau Valentine in Dressage.

In 1983, the Thomas family took Debbie and Bob to Europe to buy horses. At the Hanoverian auction in Verden, Germany, they bought two: Willie the Great, a Dressage horse for Peggy, and a hunter-jumper that Debbie remembers as a very special horse. "He was named Fridolin," she recalls, "and he stood at 17.1 hands. Thoroughbreds were considered the ultimate jumpers then, but this horse was successful enough to start a warmblood trend." Debbie says Fridolin was the first horse she ever got

  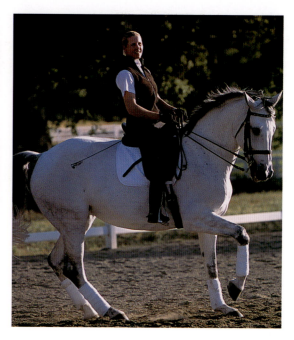

Sabine Baron on Royal Princess

to keep, and she allowed herself to bond with the animal. Perry and Peggy Thomas began buying and selling horses every year, and Debbie found it difficult to let the horses go after working closely with them.

In 1988, when Debbie was warming up a green hunter over a two-foot fence on a racetrack, a tragic accident changed the course of her career. A water truck spooked the young horse and it reared, flipping all the way over and landing on top of Debbie. She was seriously injured, with fractured ribs, a punctured spleen, and permanent damage to her female organs. While Debbie was healing she thought about her responsibility to take care of her son, and about the hardship it would cause her family if she were not there. When she began riding again, she was no longer comfortable taking jumps and risking injury. "Every time I left the ground for the next year," Debbie says, "I wondered if I would land safely on the other side. Bob told me I was getting so safe that I was heading for a big wreck."

The Thomases were also concerned, and the three wanted her to switch to riding Dressage. They took Bob and Debbie to auction in Europe to find a Dressage horse for Debbie. "We decided on a 'tryer' named Beau Rivage," Debbie recalls, "because I didn't want to spend too much starting out." The rest, as they say, is history. Debbie trained Beau Rivage, and then competed with the horse all the way to the Grand Prix level. The two represented the United States at the World Cup in Sweden in 1998.

At the 1999 Pan American Games, Debbie, riding Brentina, took an individual and a team Gold Medal. The win gave the USET its first double-gold medallist in the sport at this competition since 1983. As a result of her accomplishments, Debbie was named AHSA Equestrian of the Year and USOC Female Equestrian Athlete of the Year. In 2002,

the pair won the U.S. Freestyle Championship and the World Cup Dressage U.S. League Final in California. Next, Debbie set a goal to compete in the World Equestrian Games in Jerez de la Frontera, Spain in 2002. Debbie qualified for the World Games after winning the USET Grand Prix Championship at the selection trials at team headquarters in Gladstone, New Jersey, in the spring of 2002.

In Spain, the U.S. Dressage team won a Silver Medal. Despite a flawless demonstration of skill and preparation in the Freestyle competition, Debbie took an individual fourth place. After dismounting, she hugged Brentina and then Bob. Debbie was happy with Brentina's spectacular performance, but couldn't help feeling somewhat let down. "At the beginning," Debbie explains, "you might not have hoped to go that far. But then you find yourself in a medal situation, and your heart gets involved in it. You have hope." For Debbie, the pain of disappointment is overshadowed by the magnitude of the achievement. "I realize that to be fourth in the world is quite an

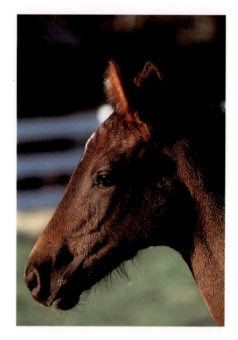

accomplishment," she says, "not only for yourself, but for America."

Her Olympic trainer is Klaus Balkenhol, who competed on many Olympic teams before he retired. Once the coach for Germany's team, he took an interest in the U.S. competitors and began coaching for the USET in 2002. Debbie has also trained with Hilda Gurney, Lilo Fore, and German Olympic Bronze Medallist, Steffen Peters. Her current goal is to compete in the 2004 Olympic Games in Athens.

"It takes a lot of hard work to be a champion," she says, "and it takes financial backing. The people behind you, and the ones behind the scenes, are so wonderful. Grooms, for example, give up their lives, basically, to go on the road with you." Debbie says it takes many such behind-the-scenes people to be a winning competitor. She considers the veterinarians at Sawtooth Equine, and her farrier, Roger Wilkenson, to be as much a part of the winning combination as Brentina and herself. "Without a good vet, you don't have a good horse. Sponsors support you financially and emotionally. And without the support of Bob, Ryan, Kim and the Thomases, it would be impossible for me to do what I'm doing."

Crooked Willow Farms,
Colorado

The History of Show Jumping

For centuries, humans found advantages in the inherent abilities of the horse to haul heavy loads and to maneuver swiftly in battle. The Greek commander Xenophon instructed cavalrymen how to jump ditches, banks and hedges in the fourth century BC, but the horse's natural ability to jump over obstacles was not especially valued until the Enclosure Acts of seventeenth-century England. The acts called for the partitioning of farming and grazing lands that were once communal, and hedges and fences suddenly dotted the English countryside for the first time. Horses were used both for hunting and for pleasure riding, particularly among members of the landed gentry. Jumping creeks, logs, hedges and stone walls became a thrilling element of the English foxhunt, and initiated the birth of a new sport.

Although horse shows in Europe and the United States date back many centuries, the first formal Show Jumping competition on record was held in 1866 at a harness horse show in Paris. In 1868, the Dublin Horse Show first included jumping as an event. In early European Show Jumping competitions, horses and riders appeared in front of spectators, and then

left the show arena to jump cross-country obstacles. For the benefit of spectators, jumps were introduced in the arena. Arena jumping became known as "lepping." The most prestigious shows included Lepping classes by 1900, although they attracted only a handful of competitors. Women riding sidesaddle competed in separate classes.

Frederico Caprilli (1868-1907) was an Italian cavalry officer whose ideas greatly modified Show Jumping. Caprilli observed horses jumping without riders, and he came to believe that when a rider inclined backward, as was the common practice of the day, the horse's natural movement was hindered. From these observations, he developed a new rider position – the forward seat. He developed a new type of saddle as well. The forward seat for jumping gradually was accepted by all major schools of horsemanship.

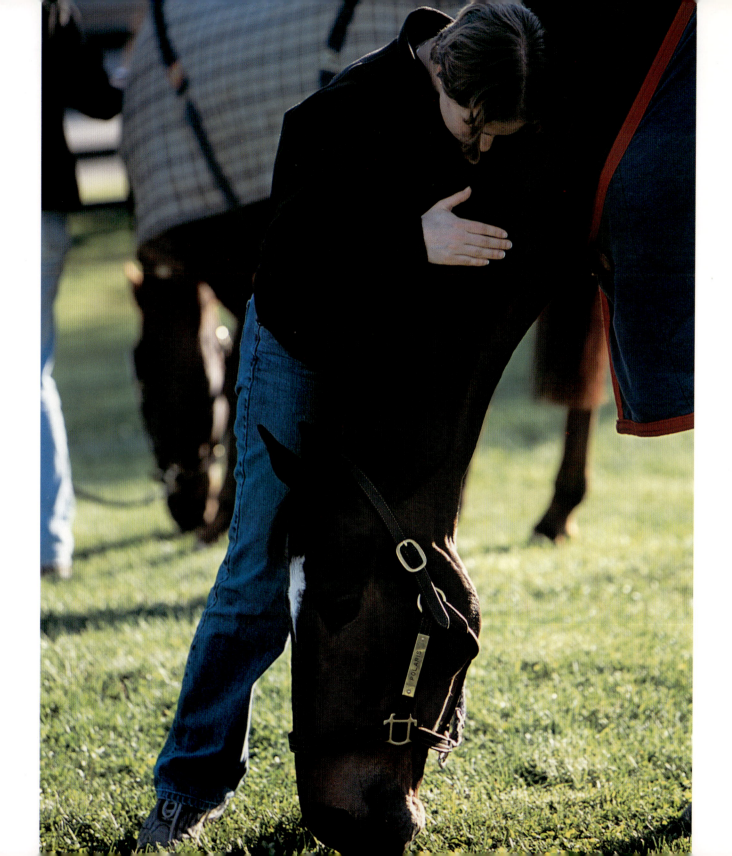

Nineteenth century horse shows were primarily national events but sometimes included competitors from neighboring countries. The first international horse show was held in 1900 at the World's Fair in Paris, where Olympic equestrian competition was held. The Societe Hippique Francaise extended its annual Concours Hippiques Central from May 29 through June 1, and high jump, long jump and Grand Prix competitions were held. Top riders from France and Belgium competed, along with Count Trissino of Italy.

In 1902, the Societa Nazionale Zootecnica organized an international horse show in Turin, Italy. One hundred forty-seven riders from six countries competed. Most of the competitors were Italian, but the German Emperor, the Austrian-Hungarian Empire, Russia,

~43

France and Belgium also sent teams. The German and Russian teams ended with poor results, hence no German army officer was allowed abroad again until 1911, and Russia changed to Caprilli's training style. The success of the 1902 competition in Turin sparked international horse shows in Lisbon, Madrid, Rome, Paris, Brussels, Den Haag, London, Lucerne, New York and Chicago. The 1912 Olympic Games in Stockholm were the first to include an equestrian program, which included Jumping, Dressage and Eventing.

George Morris' Hunterdon

From the earliest days of international equestrian competitions, it was recognized that standardized rules were necessary. In 1921, members of the Fédération Equestre Internationale (FEI) met to draft international rules for competition. In the 1930s, military jumping teams competed with one another at major equestrian events throughout Europe and North America. More than 200 Nations' Cup competitions were held from 1920-1942, in which Italy and Germany had the most wins. After 1955 the FEI allowed only one Nations' Cup per country.

By that time, most competitors were civilians. For three decades, sixteen annual Nations' Cup events were held. More were added in the late 1980s, and by 1997 the number had increased to twenty-eight.

In 1965, the FEI introduced the Presidents Cup, an annual ranking of participating countries according to their accumulative Nations' Cup results. 1968 was a winning year for Americans when the U.S. won six Nations' Cups. In international competition, American show jumpers have a proud record. At World Championships, United States Equestrian Team show jumpers won team and individual Bronze Medals in 1978, and a team Gold and individual Silver Medal in 1986. USET riders also have won seven FEI Show Jumping World Cup Finals. In addition to

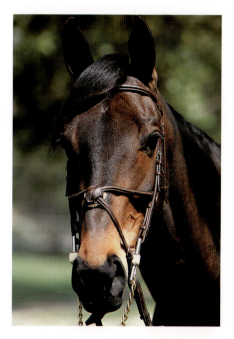

the equestrian expertise found among U.S. trainers, many European trainers have lent their expertise to USET Show Jumping teams.

Equestrian events are the only Olympic competition in which men and women compete on an equal basis. In the Olympic Games, individual Gold Medals have been won by Bill Steinkraus (1968) and Joe Fargis (1984). The U.S. also won a team Gold in 1984. The success of American riders at the 1984 Los Angeles Olympics, 1988 Seoul, 1992 Barcelona Olympics, and 1996 Atlanta Olympics brought more interest in Show Jumping.

The sights and sounds of today's Show Jumping events hint at the roots of the sport. Competitors don the traditional attire of black leather boots, hunt coat, breeches, a shirt with a tie or stock tie, and a hunt cap. Since the first competition was held in Europe a century and a half ago, the popularity of the sport has continued to grow. Perhaps much of the appeal of Show Jumping is that it evokes images of a gracious era in which finely honed equestrian skills suggested not only a love of the outdoors, but also talent, refinement, intelligence, and an advanced civilization.

~49

Competitive Show Jumping

Nicki Simpson on Falcone

The talent and the intensity necessary to succeed in Show Jumping at the advanced levels have made the sport popular with both competitors and spectators for more than a century. The challenge for riders is difficult, but straightforward. Competitors strive to jump a course of fifteen to twenty obstacles, up to five feet in height and six feet in width, without incurring penalties. Penalties, or faults, are added if a horse refuses to jump, falls, or knocks down an obstacle or jump. Each course also has a time limit. In addition to jumping faults, penalties can also accumulate if riders fail to complete the course at a certain speed or within the time allowed.

Competitors must negotiate obstacles at the correct angle, height, and speed in order to cover the course without incurring faults, and must also be mindful of the clock. The rider who races too fast may grow careless and knock down a fence, while an overly cautious rider may incur time faults. The starting order of riders is determined by a draw before the event so that each rider has an equal chance of attaining a favorable position. Competitors near the end of the starting order have the advantage of seeing how earlier riders completed

Nicki Simpson on Petri at the Show Park Grand Prix, San Diego

the course.

Riders preview the course by walking it on foot prior to the competition. This is the only chance the rider has to study the course up close. Each competitor knows the length of his horse's stride, and he or she walks the course accordingly, pacing off the distance between fences, and determining how best to adjust the horse's strides. Riders take note of the different types of fences offered as well as their relationships to one another, the footing, and any other potential problem areas. They also look for places where a tighter path could save vital time. The following types of jumps are common in competition:

Vertical – *These are straight up and down fences with no spread width. These appear simple but are some of the most difficult for the horse to jump.*

The Wall – These solid-looking jumps have top sections that can be dislodged, which would result in faults.

Oxers – Two elements are combined in one jump to create a spread. Parallel oxers present the most difficulty.

Triple Bar – These are spread fences with three elements of graduating height. This makes the jump very wide, although the fences are each relatively easy to jump.

Combination – This is a series of two or more fences placed one or two strides apart. A refusal of any fence requires the horse and rider to re-jump the entire combination.

Water Jump – These are broad jumps of 12 to 16 feet. A low hedge or fence usually marks the leading edge. The horse must clear the tape on the far side of the jump or the rider will incur jumping faults.

Competition at the Show Park Grand Prix, San Diego

Gate – *These vertical jumps are made to appear solid using planks, gates, brush or balustrades.*

All jumper classes are subject to the same scoring systems. The winner is the horse and rider team with the fewest jumping and time penalties. All obstacles are numbered, and horse and rider must take the course in a designated sequence. Each rider's goal is to cover the course without faults within the allotted time period. Style is not taken into account, and it does not affect the scoring. If a horse refuses a jump, the penalty is three faults for the first time. Six faults are given for a second refusal, and a third results in elimination. A penalty of four faults is incurred each time a fence is knocked down, and the penalty for a horse touching the water at a water jump is also four faults. Exceeding the time allowed to complete the

Mary Tyng at the Show Park Grand Prix, San Diego

course results in penalties as well. Frequently, several horses complete the course without penalties. These riders advance to a jump-off over a shortened course. In the case of equal faults during the jump-off, the horse and rider team with the fastest time will be declared the winner.

International Show Jumping competitions are governed by the Federation Equestre Internationale (FEI), which sets forth rules and regulations. At the international level there are five levels of competition: Prix St George, Intermediaire I, Intermediaire II, Grand Prix, and the highest level, Grand Prix Special. The French term "Grand Prix" means "richest or greatest prize." The term is often used to designate the most challenging or sophisticated level of competition in a particular sport.

No two Grand Prix courses are the same. The course designer's goal is to provide a challenging course that only a few horses can complete without incurring faults. Using a variety of colors, types and combinations of jumps, course designers alter the courses according to the level of competition. At all levels of competition, Show Jumping requires skill, strategic planning and seamless cooperation between horse and rider.[1]

[1] Description provided by the United States Equestrian Team, 2002.

Mandy Porter at the Show Park Grand Prix, San Diego

George Morris

An American Legend in Show Jumping

George Morris is a renowned equestrian trainer whose remarkable career as a rider includes winning a Pan American Gold Medal in Show Jumping in 1959 as well as a Silver Medal at the 1960 Olympic games in Rome. He has been a member of eight Nations' Cup winning teams. Morris began teaching equitation in 1964. His former students have enjoyed marked success in international Show Jumping. They include Olympic Gold medallists Conrad Homfeld, Melanie Smith Taylor and Leslie Burr Howard, and silver medallists Lisa Jacquin, Anne Kursinski and Peter Leone. He serves on the AHSA Board of Directors, and is president of the Show Jumping Hall of Fame. A member of the USET Executive and Show Jumping Committees, he is also the organization's Vice President for Show Jumping. His career has been illustrative of his exceptional talent and steadfast dedication to the sport.

Morris was born in New York City in 1938, and grew up in the lush, green countryside of New Canaan, Connecticut. "I was always horse crazy," he says. "Initially, I loved horses and ponies, and eventually,

George Morris working with student

I loved riding." His family owned a horse they used for transportation both during the Depression and during WW II. Morris describes it as "roguey" and difficult, but the horse's less than admirable disposition didn't dissuade the youngster from his love of animals. He remembers having one hundred stuffed animals in his room as a boy, and still describes himself as "an animal nut."

A timid child, and initially, a timid rider, Morris joined the New Canaan Mounted Troop at the age of seven. The New Canaan group was formed during World War II, and the boys wore uniforms and drilled both on foot and on horseback. Although Morris didn't care for the marching, he enjoyed the opportunity to ride. After about six months, his family sent him to the Ox Ridge Hunt Club in Darien, Connecticut.

The renowned club, which is still in existence, held a big show every summer. It was there that Morris had his first taste of competition, in 1948. A preview of his illustrious career, he took blue ribbons in his first jumping and equitation classes.

Richard Spooner at Indio, California

Morris believes much of his success is owed to the training he received in his early career, and the fact that he didn't start riding too young. As a rule, he believes, starting a rider at three or four years old can be detrimental. Having the right start, he says, has a great impact on a rider's future success. "In your career," says Morris, "you should have three principle teachers: a great starting teacher, a great technical teacher, and a world-class trainer. I was lucky. I had all of those."

An Englishwoman named Felicia Townsend was Morris's beginning instructor. "She gave people great confidence, and helped them develop a

wonderful rapport with horses," he recalls. Morris says Townsend gave him an excellent start in basic riding and position. Also at Ox Ridge, Morris came under the tutelage of a German instructor named Otto Heuckeroth. "He added 'blood and guts' to your start," he remembers.

Although he feels that Townsend and Heuckeroth were a good combination for a beginner, the instruction wasn't advanced enough to go on with the finer details of riding and showing. Luckily, Morris says, only a half-hour from New Canaan in White Plains, New York, was the greatest instructor in the country: Gordon Wright. The better young riders from Ox Ridge went to take lessons with him once or twice weekly. Wright was a top-notch horseman from the Ft. Riley, Kansas Calvary School. "He took me on, and he gave me a great technical base," Morris says.

Morris's family owned a large New York newspaper. Although they supported his riding, they insisted that his schoolwork was a priority.

"My grandmother was a stickler for grades," he remembers. "It was just a fact that if I wasn't on the honor roll, I wouldn't have the horses." His family bought him a wonderful competition horse called Gamecock, which he rode in junior hunter and equitation classes.

Morris caught the attention of the equestrian world in 1952 when, at the age of fourteen, he won two of the nation's most prestigious competitions for young riders: the AHSA Medal Class and the ASPCA McClay Class at Madison Square Gardens. He is still the youngest competitor on record to have ever won both of the prominent contests, a feat he attributes to a great horse, and to the excellent instruction of Gordon Wright.

Anke Magnussen with Crescendo at Royal Oaks Farm, California

"They were beautiful and prestigious trophies," Morris says. "This was a wonderful weekend, but at the same time, it had its drawbacks. There was an unwritten rule that if you won these two classes, you should no longer compete in junior events." Because he had completed two legs on some challenge trophies that had to be won three times, he continued to compete for about seven months. By the middle of his fifteenth year, Morris had wrapped up his junior career three years earlier than most junior riders. For young riders like Morris, a vacuum is created in similar situations, he says, much to the frustration of competitors and professional trainers.

Morris turned to open jumper riding during the void. He sold his wonderful horse, Gamecock, and he bought a green open jumper named Gigolo in 1953. He began showing the horse in green open jumper competitions in 1954, and by 1955, they were winning some important shows. When he was seventeen, Morris won a big open jumper class at Madison Square Gardens, and he had his eye on the Olympic Games.

Morris saw his precocious career as a detriment. "Everything happened to me too soon," he reflects. "It's not best when things are too much, too easy, and too soon. You're not quite ready for what is happening." At eighteen, Morris bought War Bride, a granddaughter of Man O' War, as well as two other good horses. He tried out for the Stockholm Olympics in 1956. In scoring, he came in just behind Bill Steinkraus, but he did not make the team. "The committee, rightfully, decided I didn't have the experience," Morris recalls. He was heartbroken,

~71

he says, and his family was very disappointed, although in reflection, Morris sees it as the right decision. "It was very good, because I was not prepared to go to Stockholm," he says. "There is a lot of discussion today about subjective and objective, and I know both sides of the coin because I've been there. The decision to compete when you're too young doesn't do you any good because there are voids in your career. There is much pressure, and it's simply too much, too soon."

After the 1956 Olympics, Morris was invited to ride with the United States Equestrian Team on an informal basis. He had started college at the University of Virginia in 1957, but transferred to Columbia University because it was closer to USET headquarters. Morris felt he was close to realizing his dream of getting on the Olympic squad, and he missed nearly two months of classes at Columbia while riding with the team. In his absence, his girlfriend took his exams, and the school did not know he wasn't attending. He left Columbia after the first semester, and never returned to college.

Morris realized his goal of riding with the U.S. Equestrian Team, and had three wonderful tours in Europe, including the 1960 Olympic Games in Rome. "Competing in the Olympics is like no other competition," he says. "The weight of the country – the world – is on you. The fences, the courses, are the most difficult you've ever jumped, but it's like no other experience. It's one you never forget." On a good horse called Sinjon, Morris did better than he expected. He took second place in the team class, and won a fourth place individual medal.

In that era competitors had to be pure amateurs, but after the Olympics, Morris says he felt it was time to make a living. He was twenty-two years old. "I had no skills to earn a living," he remembers, "but in those days, it was not 'kosher' for a WASP from New Canaan, Connecticut, with a social register background to go into the horse business." His family didn't like the idea so he tried another career, spending two years at a New York theater school called The Neighborhood Playhouse. He graduated in 1962, and did little riding for two years. He worked at acting jobs in summer stock and on television with the help of a great agent – a family friend who represented only four actors: Montgomery Cliff, Marlon Brando, Grace Kelly, and Morris. When he was offered a five-year Hollywood studio contract with Warner Brothers, he thought hard about the opportunity. Under such contracts, an actor couldn't work for anyone but the studio. "You could end up a superstar, or a nobody," Morris says. "I didn't have enough special attributes to be a James Dean." His agent, a fellow rider from Ox Ridge, wanted him to stay with horses. Morris came to the same

decision. His acting experience, he believes, later proved valuable in his teaching career when he was required to stand on his feet and speak for hours.

In 1963, he spent a year studying dressage with Gerner Anderson, an Olympic trainer of the highest reputation. Morris felt he needed to come back into the horse world as a professional, however, in fairness to his family and to himself. "They had always supported me," Morris says, "and I just couldn't ask them for more." In 1964, at twenty-six, he hung out his shingle as a professional trainer.

Almost immediately, he attracted good clients. When one of his students, Jimmy Kohn, won the Medal Finals at Madison Square Gardens, Morris was catapulted to the forefront as a top trainer. From 1964 to 1984 he trained equitation and hunter riders, and many of his students went on to make the Olympic team and became World Finals champions. For twenty years, he dedicated his life to young people. Morris feels that one element of his success as a trainer is that he was not a natural rider. "You're better off if you had to struggle as a rider," he says. "Otherwise, you don't know the pitfalls of an average rider."

In 1983, Morris's career took an interesting turn. Although he hadn't ridden Grand Prix horses for twenty years, he started riding once more. He had bought some young and talented horses in the 1980s, and they drew him back to Grand Prix competition. "It was great fun," Morris says.

"I was forty-five when I started." In 1988, Morris won the biggest purse in Show Jumping history while competing on a horse called Rio at Spruce Meadows, Canada. His ten-year renaissance lasted from 1983 to 1993. "It was most unexpected," he remembers. "I just got so excited about these young horses. I was having a blast. People in California who watched me at shows were saying, 'Is that the same George Morris? The one who gives clinics here?'"

Morris, now in his mid-sixties, hasn't competed much in the last ten years. "There's a time to quit," he says. "You get older, and your bones break more easily." Morris still jumps, but he has plenty of other activities that keep him busy. He has served as Chef d'Equipe of the U.S. Olympic Jumping Team several times, and is chairman of the Show Jumping Committee. He focuses on his private students, gives talks and clinics, and has shared his vast expertise in books he has written. Morris's first book, Hunter Seat Equitation, is in its third edition. His most recent book, The American Jumping Style, chronicles the development and establishment of the American forward seat as a worldwide influence.

Morris also spends time with his family and friends at his longtime home, Hunterdon, located in Pittstown, New Jersey. He also enjoys a lovely home in Florida.

And then, of course, he continues to look for good horses. "When you're a horseman," he says, "you are always looking for that perfect horse."

~75

Three-Day Event History

David O'Connor at the
Rolex 3-Day Event, 2002

Three-day Event has its roots in the equestrian training programs of the military. When the sport was first introduced at the 1912 Olympic Games, participation was limited to army officers. The difficult circumstances military horses and cavalrymen encountered in the field required equestrian abilities that were far more demanding than in any other venue. Obedience, speed, stamina, bravery and versatility were required of the cavalry charger, and less than excellent horsemanship on the part of mounted soldiers could result in injury, the loss of a battle, or death. The earliest traditions of equestrian training, dating back more than four thousand years, were designed to meet the unique requirements of horsemanship during a battle.

In Germany, the sport is still called the "Militaire," while Americans sometimes use the term, "Combined Training." The British called the competition Three-day Event because the competition takes place over three consecutive days. Each phase of the competition represents a function of military equestrianship and a challenging test for the army horse. The Dressage Test given on the first day of the event mirrors the precision and elegance necessary on the parade ground. The second day of the event involves the Endurance

Karen O'Connor on Grand Slam at the Rolex 3-Day Event, 2002

Test, which includes a short Roads and Tracks (Phase A), followed immediately by a Steeplechase (Phase B), and then a long Roads and Tracks (Phase C). A compulsory halt of ten minutes allows time for a veterinary examination, after which the competitor begins the Cross-Country (Phase D). In earlier days, there was an additional Phase E on the second day, which included a 1.0-mile flat run after the Cross-Country. Today, this phase is no longer included. On the third day, riders compete in the Jumping Test in which they must negotiate a series of obstacles over an 800-meter course.

In the grueling Olympic Games competition in Stockholm in 1912, only fifteen of the twenty-seven starting competitors finished. Captain Guy V. Henry, Jr., served as coach for the five officers and eighteen horses that made up the United States Equestrian Team. After training at Fort Riley, Kansas, the team sailed across the Atlantic for fifteen days. With little exercise, the horses arrived soft and sluggish. Although the team had only thirteen days to prepare for the strenuous trials ahead of them, the U.S. finished with a Bronze Medal.

Bruce Davidson at the Rolex 3-Day Event, 2002

The format used today in Three-day Event competition was established at the 1924 Olympic Games in Paris. This was the first time the event was open to

David O'Connor on The Native heading for the water

~81

civilians. The U.S. was the only non-European nation that competed. International rules for the Three-day Event are designated by the *Fédération Equestre Internationale* (FEI). The FEI states that the object of the performance is to "show the rider's spirit, boldness, and perfect knowledge of his horse's paces and their use across country, and to show the condition, handiness, courage, jumping ability, stamina, and speed of the well trained horse."

The U.S. Army's official participation in Olympic equestrian events ended in 1948 at the Olympic Games in London. Women riders were not allowed to compete in eventing until 1964. U.S. teams have been a dominant force from the event's beginning. American eventers brought home team Gold Medals at the 1976 and 1984 Olympic Games, and David O'Connor won an individual Gold at the 2000 Olympic Games in Sydney. In 2002, the U.S. Eventing team won its first World Championship Gold Medal at the World Equestrian Games in Spain.

Three-day eventing remained popular throughout the twentieth century, and today, the popularity of the sport continues to grow. In Olympic Games and World Championship competitions, the most advanced abilities of horse and rider are required. Individuals and international teams represent their home countries, and vie for international prestige as well as individual achievement.

Darren Chiacchia at the Rolex 3-Day Event, 2002

Three-Day Eventing in Competition

Darrah Alexander on Brimestone
at the Rolex 3-Day Event, 2002

The Three-day Event is a challenging test of a horse and rider's skill and all-around ability, and is the ultimate test of teamwork between the two. Three-day eventing features four levels of competition which, in increasing levels of difficulty, are designated by one, two, three, or four stars. Horses and riders must earn the right to compete at these levels. At each successive level a horse has to jump higher and run farther and faster, therefore it must have more trust in the rider at each level. The degree of difficulty for gymnastic exercises increases progressively on the flat, in the Dressage phase, and over fences during the cross-country test.

Olivia Bunn on GV Top of the Line

The First Phase:
DRESSAGE COMPETITION

The Dressage test in three-day eventing reflects the cavalry officer's need for an obedient, attractive mount on the parade ground. The objective, as is always the case in dressage, is to demonstrate a harmonious development of the horse's physique and balance. Each horse and rider combination is required to perform a prescribed set of movements within a confined area. Three independent judges award marks ranging from 0 to 10 for each movement. Collective marks are given for the horse's pace, impulsion and submission to the rider's directions, as well as for the rider's position and use of aids. The test must be executed from memory. Errors or incorrect sequences of movements result in point penalties.

Throughout the Dressage test judges look for calmness and relaxation combined with impulsion and rhythm. The horse should be at the peak of fitness, and yet still full of energy for the strenuous demands of the remaining competition. A Dressage performance should be fluid, balanced and accurate, providing an overall picture of grace and harmony. Many years of training are required to produce a well-schooled horse that can perform a good Dressage test. Without the obedience and suppleness Dressage requires, the cross-country and jumping phases would be considerably more difficult.

The Second Phase:
SPEED AND ENDURANCE TEST

The speed and endurance test is the most exciting and challenging part of a Three-day Event. It consists of four parts: two sessions of Roads and Tracks, a Steeplechase, and a Cross-Country Test with as many as thirty obstacles placed in a varied terrain. The obstacles must be jumped boldly and with speed. Some obstacles may include four or five separate jumping efforts.

When casual observers think of eventing, they usually envision the thrilling Cross-Country test. Yet each portion of the Speed and Endurance test proves the rider's knowledge of pace and use of the horse across country. Competitors must complete the Speed and Endurance test within a prescribed "optimum time." Time penalties will be incurred if the competitor takes the course is taken too slowly, and exceeds the optimum time. The four separate phases are individually timed, each requiring a different speed and each offering varied and specific challenges. Under adverse conditions of weather or terrain, phase lengths and times allowed may be altered for safety reasons. In the Cross-Country phase, in addition to time penalties, penalties are also incurred for jumping faults such as refusals and run-outs.

Kim Vinoski on Winsome Adante at the Rolex 3-Day Event, 2002

The Third Phase:
SHOW JUMPING

The final component of a Three-day Event is the Stadium-Jumping phase. In order to compete, horses must pass a series of veterinary inspections after the Speed and Endurance phase. Show Jumping tests the horse's ability to retain the suppleness, energy and obedience necessary to complete a jumping course after their great efforts of the previous day. The object is to complete the course, which consists of various colored, moveable obstacles, without incurring penalties from knockdowns, refusals, falls or exceeding the time limit.

The overall winners of a Three-day Event are determined by converting Dressage scores to penalties, and then adding the penalties incurred in Speed and Endurance and Show Jumping. The competitor with the lowest number of penalties wins. Three-day Eventing demands versatility of talent and excellent physical condition in both horse and rider as well as horsemanship abilities of the highest order. Top-level Three-day Event competitors, both equine and human, represent the finest examples of excellence in the equestrian world. [1]

[1] Description provided by the United States Equestrian Team, 2002.

Bruce Davidson making it look easy
at the Rolex 3-day Event, 2002

Captain Mark Phillips
Chef d'Equipe of the U.S. Eventing Team

Captain Mark Phillips became Chef d'Equipe and Technical Advisor for the United States Equestrian Team Eventing squad in 1993. Under his leadership, U.S. Eventing teams have regained a position of international prominence, including medal winning performances at the 1994 and 1998 World Equestrian Games, the 1995 and 1999 Pan American Games, the 1996 Olympic Games, and the 2000 Olympic Games, where David O'Connor won the individual Gold. The U.S. Eventing Team became world champions when they brought home the team Gold at the 2002 World Equestrian Games. The USET has ranked among the world's top three teams continually since Phillips' involvement, and his commitment to the team has been extended through the 2004 Athens Olympics.

A native of Great Britain, Phillips began his successful equestrian career as a youth when he rode for the Beaufort Hunt Pony Club Team for five years. His notable competitive career includes representing Great Britain in the Show Jumping arena on two winning Nations' Cup teams, and winning team Gold Medals at the 1972 Olympic Games and the World and

Captain Mark & Sandy Phillips working with Karen O'Conner at the Rolex 3-Day Event

European Championships. His accomplishments also include a win at Burghley and four wins at Badminton. Phillips retired from international competition after riding with the British Three-day Event Olympic Team that won the Silver Medal at the 1988 Olympic Games in Seoul. Since then, he has devoted his time to teaching, designing courses, and writing.

Phillips' love of riding began when he was a child. "I was lucky enough to have parents who helped me ride when I was a kid," he says. "I had a pony, and I was in the Pony Club. My hobby became my sport, and my profession." As he realized some successes showing ponies, his horizons expanded. Eventually, he was showing horses and winning championships. "I didn't say to myself at eight years old, 'I want to ride in the Olympics,'"

William Fox-Pitt on Stunning at the Rolex 3-Day Event, 2002

Phillips says. "That wasn't how it went. One thing led to another."

While he was involved in the Pony Club, Phillips trained in Dressage, Show Jumping and Cross-Country. "One thing I enjoyed doing as a kid and as a teenager was galloping and jumping fences," he remembers. "I then had to learn how to trot in circles for the Dressage, and how to jump colored poles." The training he received at the Pony Club would prove to be a solid base for a lifetime dedicated to horsemanship.

Phillips joined the Queen's Dragoon Guards in 1969, and served in the army until 1978. He won the Badminton Horse Trials in 1971 and 1972 riding Great Ovation. He won the prestigious competition again in 1974 on Queen Elizabeth the Queen Mother's horse, Columbus, and won at Badmiton a fourth time on Lincoln, in 1981. Phillips remembers Columbus as the best horse he ever rode. "He was a superb athlete. He could take off from far away or close. He could put in four strides in a combination, or one stride in a combination," Phillips says. "Riding

him, you had all the aces – you could solve a problem two or three different ways." The horse, he recalls, seemed to perform best when the pressure was on. "I think some horses are better at rising to the occasion. They appreciate a big occasion, and they perform better at big events."

Phillips says he has had both good and bad relationships with horses, and with dogs as well, and he values the good alliances he has had. "One of the important aspects of the sport," he says, "is the relationship that riders are able to develop with an animal." Phillips believes the high level of concern most riders and owners feel toward their horses is often overlooked by outsiders. "One of the things that is seldom covered is the unbelievable care and attention that goes into looking after these horses, before, during and after a competition," he says. "The affection, the bond, the care – the way these horses are looked after is unbelievable. The bond and affection between a horse and rider is a special part of the sport."

Eventing is a challenging test of equestrian abilities, and is designed to test the fitness and the versatility of the horse as well. Phillips believes

Eventing horses must be special athletes. "They have to be calm and obedient in the Dressage, while at the same time, as fit as a racehorse," he says. "They have to have the speed and endurance to gallop and jump all day in the cross-country, be brave enough to take a few rubs on the course, and yet careful enough to leave the colored poles up on the last day". To find a horse and a rider good in all three phases, he says, is a fairly rare combination.

Phillips' winning record proved him to be one of those rare equestrians. Although he had won several important national and world contests, he believes winning a Gold Medal at the 1972 Olympic Games was the highlight of his competitive career," "I think the Olympic Games is the pinnacle of any athlete's career, " he says. "You can win national championships, and you can win international competitions, but the Olympic Games is different. When you are standing on that podium, and you see your national flag go up,

Twist & Shout with handler at the Rolex 3-Day Event, 2002

~101

that's a special moment in any athlete's career."

Riders who compete in Three-day Event share a common love for the exhilarating rush of the cross-country, and they share a common bond, Phillips says, with other competitors. "In the Three-day event, you're on a thousand pounds of horse, galloping at twenty -five miles per hour over four feet of fixed timber. The danger element in that creates a special bond and a unique atmosphere and friendship amongst the people who share those dangers." Winning is a tremendous thrill, but Phillips says there are a lot more disappointments than successes. "It makes people appreciate success if it comes," he says, "and it makes competitors genuinely happy for those who manage to succeed."

In addition to his other accomplishments, Phillips is a respected course designer, and is known for building courses that are both challenging and safe for horses. He is the AHSA/USCTA National Course Advisor, and has designed several top-level courses. Phillips believes that safety is the most important element in course design. "You are always trying to make the fences as safe as possible for the horses, even if the rider makes a mistake," he says, but adds that with safety there are sometimes consequences. "We made the fences safer for the horses, and we began to lose riders. I believe that one of the reasons that happens is that when fences are safer for horses, people are able to upgrade to levels above their riding competence." Those who compete in Three-day Event, he believes, are keenly aware of the risks. "It's something everybody accepts," he says, "We train to minimize those risks. That's what training is all about."

In September 2002, the United States Eventing Team won the Gold Medal at the 2002 World Equestrian Games in Jerez de la Frontera, Spain. It was the first time in twenty-eight years the team had won a world championship, and all members expressed gratitude for Phillips' guidance as Chef d'Equipe. "Right now, the sport is a success story in this country," Phillips says. "Anytime the national team does well, in any country in the world, the sport grows because people like to be involved with success."

In Phillips' mind, however, success is no reason to stop striving for improvement, and for progression to new levels. "The day you stop learning is the day you die," he says. "The only way you get better is to always have an open mind to learning and trying new things. Nothing is forever. Nothing stands still in this life. There is only progress." He believes that the ability and the willingness to learn is an important part of keeping up with the sport, and is vital to being in the front line. In a discipline as steeped in tradition as Three-day Eventing, Phillips' progressive philosophy may be the thing that has given him, and the USET Eventing Team, a winning edge.

Early morning at the Kentucky Horse Park, Lexington, Kentucky

Crooked Willow Farms, Colorado

The History of Combined Driving

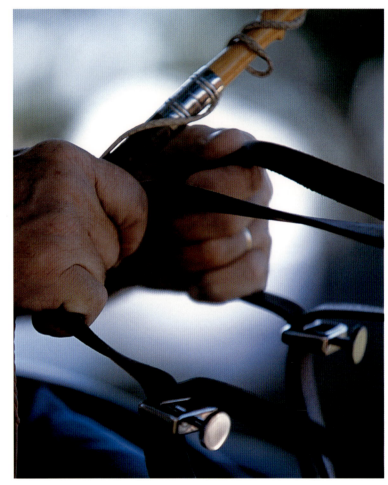

Most Paleo-historians believe the earliest civilizations that tamed horses used them to pull carts before learning to ride them. In the Middle East, hoofed animals such as oxen and asses had been harnessed to carts long before horses were domesticated. Nearly two millennia ago, the Hittites invented the war chariot and, as a result, were able to conquer Egypt and Mesopotamia. These fast chariots carried one man who drove and another who fought. Chariot racing was established as an equestrian sport in both the Greek and Roman circuses, and was a part of the early Olympic Games. A mounted cavalry had developed in most civilizations by about 100 A.D., and chariotry quickly disappeared as a means of warfare. Most archaeological evidence suggests not only that people harnessed horses long before riding developed, but also that horsemanship spread from the Near East to Europe and the steppes.

For centuries, most driving was done with carts or wagons that hauled goods from the fields to the marketplace. During the 1600s, however, carriages became popular among the upper classes in

Warming up for the Driving Competition in Gladstone, New Jersey

Europe. In 1899, a German driver, Benno von Achenbach (1861-1936) published Principles of Harnessing and Driving. Von Achenbach's guidelines for Driving soon became the accepted standard.

In early times, the competitions that tested individual aspects of the sport usually were held as separate events. Dressage competitions focused on elegance, and were aptly called Concours d'Elegance, while long distance competitions tested stamina and obstacle courses tested maneuverability. In 1969, the *Fédération Equestre Internationale* (FEI) accepted driving as an official discipline. A rules and regulations committee designed the rules in the fall of 1969 at the Swiss Cavalry school in Bern. They adopted the Three-day Event model, and combined the three aspects of

Harde Zantke warming up the team

Driving: Dressage, Cross-country Marathon, and the Obstacle Course.

The rules were implemented for the first time at the Royal Windsor Horse Show. The event was sponsored by Prince Philip, who remains a strong supporter of Combined Driving. During the first ten years, only competitions for Four-in-Hand teams were held at FEI driving events. In the early 1980s, competitions for pairs of horses were added, and later, competitions for single horses were added as well. Today, there are also events for Pony Driving. Four-in-Hand competition, however, remains in the forefront of international Combined Driving events.

Until 2002, the best finish for a U.S. Four-in-Hand team at a World Championship was fourth place, which they won in 1984 and 1986. At the 2002 World Equestrian Games in Jemez de Frontera, Spain, the United States Four-in-Hand team, made up of drivers Jimmy Fairclough, Chester Weber, and Tucker Johnson, won the team Silver Medal. Although its roots are founded in equestrian pursuits that date back thousands of years, Combined Driving as a competitive sport is relatively new. The rapid growth of the sport, in numbers of both participants and spectators, has been an exciting development in equestrian sports.

~111

Combined Driving Competition

Water hazard at Gladstone, New Jersey

Until the automobile was invented and mass production made it affordable, the driven horse was the most effective and dependable means of transportation. As a competitive sport, Combined Driving is an excellent challenge for the true horse lover. The Combined Driving Event, also called the Driving Three-day Event, involves three separate phases: Dressage, Marathon and Cones. The sport demands versatility in both drivers and their horses as they compete in these three very different sections of the competition. Each phase of the three-day competition has its own specific requirements of energy, skill, precision and obedience. Competitions are held for single horses, pairs, and four-in-hand. Unlike other equestrian disciplines, drivers are separated from their horses by distance and are able to communicate with the horse only through their voices, their hands on the lines, and their cues with a whip. This adds to the challenge of Combined Driving.

Phase One
DRESSAGE TEST

The competition begins with a Dressage Test driven in a pattern that must be memorized by each competitor. This is where the driver shows off the harmonious development of the horse's physique and its ability gained through progressive levels of training. Suppleness and responsiveness are necessary for driving the Dressage Test, and the best tests will show off the horse's even, rhythmic cadence, its brilliant movement, and its correct and accurate transitions. This is the most elegant part of the competition, as both horses and drivers are "turned out" in their best. The overall impression of suitability and style is reflected in their scores. Judges evaluate competitors for cleanliness and condition of the horse, harness and carriage; the fit of harness and vehicle to the horse; the position of the driver; and the appropriateness of vehicles and horses.

Phase Two
MARATHON

The action-packed, Cross-Country test challenges the driver's judgment and skill as well as the obedience, courage and agility of the horse. It is in this phase that long hours of conditioning are put to the test over a 22-kilometer Cross-Country course. This section is pure sport, and the nostalgic elegance of the first phase is replaced by state-of-the-art vehicles and sturdy harnesses. There may be three or five sections in the Marathon. Each section is designed to be driven at a specific rate of speed. Time penalties are incurred for coming in too early or too late. The horse's energy must be carefully conserved, and overtaxing the animal in the early parts of the course may cause the horse to tire out before it gets to the obstacles. Veterinarians check the condition of the horses along the route and determine whether they are fit enough to continue to the final section of the Marathon.

A three-section Marathon consists of a trot, followed by a walk, and concludes with the Cross-Country section. A five-section Marathon has an additional trot and walk before the start of the Cross-Country.

The Cross-Country section consists of seven challenging obstacles, which must be negotiated at a high speed. The horse must be courageous, fit, and ready for anything it encounters during the Marathon. Seven obstacles along the course test the horse's agility, strength, courage and obedience as well as the skill and judgement of the driver. The obstacles present unique problems such as water crossings, tight twists through trees, and visual problems with lines of fences or narrow openings. Drivers must find the fastest route through each obstacle. During this phase, a navigator helps guide the driver through obstacles, helps balance the weight of the carriage, and assists the horse and driver with timing.

The true partnership between horses and driver is evident during the Marathon. Seasoned horses know and love the game. As time is all-important, the Hazard section becomes an exciting race. Both instinct and experience tell a driver how to navigate a Marathon course.

Phase Three
CONES COURSE

On the final day of competition, drivers return to the arena once again in formal dress. Here, they face a completely different challenge than the Dressage Test. The Cones Test was developed to demonstrate how well horses have recovered physically and mentally from the stress of the Marathon. It is a test of precision driving and timing. Drivers wind their way through a course of tightly-spaced pairs of cones, attempting to finish within the time allowed on course. Cones, which are topped by balls that topple off if the cone is struck, are set with the same wheel clearance for each competitor. At the lower levels of competition drivers are allowed 50 cm (29 inches) of clearance, but the course taken by advanced drivers allows only 25 cm, or 10 inches wider than their wheel tracks.

As in Three-Day Eventing, Combined Driving is scored by a system of penalty points and the winner is the driver with the lowest score. Although the sport is relatively new in the United States, the recent accomplishments of American Combined Driving teams in world competitions have catapulted the U.S. into a position of international prominence.[1]

[1] Description provided by the United States Equestrian Team, 2002.

~115

Hardy Zantke
Chef d'Equipe of the USET Four-in-Hand Driving Team

Hardy Zantke's humor, charm, and natural friendliness have contributed as much to his success in Combined Driving as his competitive spirit and expertise. For more than two decades he has been involved in the sport of Combined Driving at every level. A top-level competitor, he also serves on the boards of both USAEq and the United States Equestrian Team. He served as Chef d'Equipe for the U.S. Team at the 1996 Four-in-Hand World Championship in Belgium, and also for the U.S. team that brought home the team Silver Medal in the Four-in-Hand Driving World Championship in 2002. In addition to competing, coaching and training, Zantke writes for several horse magazines, holds clinics, and serves as a show judge.

He was first introduced to horses as a boy at his grandfather's house in East Germany after World War II. His grandfather operated a small trucking company, and Zantke says that after the war, it was nearly impossible to get parts to repair the company's two delivery trucks. His grandfather's six teams of draft horses reliably took over the job of pick-ups and deliveries for eight hours each day, six days a the week. It was a small city, but when making deliveries to the railroad from local merchants and light industry companies, he says speed was

not crucial. As a boy, Zantke was allowed to ride along with the teamsters. For him, the time spent with "his" teamster and with the horses was bliss. "When I was a little boy," Zantke recalls, "I spent more time in the stable than in the house."

At thirteen, when Zantke was on summer vacation from school, the teamster he often rode with became ill. "Grandpa looked at me," Zantke remembers, "and asked, 'Do you think you can handle the team by yourself?'" He was thrilled by the opportunity, and while his friends played in the street, he drove the team in the city for four weeks. "That's how I started," Zantke says, " and Grandpa and my teamster are still on the back of my carriage every day. We can't see them, but I know they are there." Later, he served a term in the West German army. During officers' training, the candidates were asked by the commanding officer to further their "gentlemen's education" by taking either formal dancing or riding lessons. Zantke says he opted for the riding lessons.

In 1969, Zantke and his wife, Jutta, came to the United States, first living in New York and Chicago before settling in Torrance, California, in the early 1970s. It was here that Zantke was reintroduced to horses. Driving was a fledgling sport in the U.S. at the time, but for Zantke it evoked his fondest childhood memories. "I didn't know much about driving as a competitive sport," he says, "but neither did anyone else at the time. I was the one-eyed leading the blind. But I have always been very competitive. Even as a newcomer, I was successful." Zantke competes mostly in pair driving.

He took lessons from a few people in the U.S. and from instructors in Germany where the sport, is much more developed. At the top level in the four-in-hand competitions, Zantke says there are probably five teams in the U.S. with the skill level to compete internationally . Germany, he says, probably has sixty such teams, all in contention with one another over who will represent the country during important events. And Germany, is not an exception. Dozens of good teams compete in France, Great Britain, the Netherlands, Denmark, Sweden, and other European countries as well. While carriage driving has developed in Europe for centuries, America's drivers are pioneering the sport in the U.S., and Zantke has been one of its greatest supporters.

He views his role as Chef d'Equipe of the USET Driving Team modestly. "It means I'm the one they come to when they need the key to the toilet," he jokes. He believes his job is to act as a liaison between competitors and show officials, and to get the athletes as acclimated to their European surroundings as possible. Zantke says he is also there to see that they have the things they need and to file any necessary protests. His role, as he sees it, is one of a team captain more than that of a trainer. He also helps to encourage teamwork among drivers who, when back in the U.S., frequently compete against one another. "Our first concern is to bring in a team medal for the U.S.," he stresses.

Zantke says Americans are at a disadvantage when competing

in Europe because of the changes in feed and climate. The team's expenses are also a drawback. It costs about $5000 per horse in airfare, and each of the three drivers takes five horses and two carriages. He estimates transportation costs for the team to be $250,000 for an event that takes place abroad. European competitors do not incur the same costs. Getting sponsorships can be difficult, Zantke says, because the sport is not yet as popular as other equine events. "Unfortunately," he says, "we have far too few spectators."

Another aspect of the sport, one in which Zantke delights, is competition for disabled drivers. He serves as Chef d'Equipe for the U.S. disabled driving team as well. Zantke says he met a girl from California who was mucking her stall from a wheelchair, and he told her about the events for disabled drivers. He soon began giving her lessons. "I teach her a little about driving, but I learn from her about life," Zantke says. "Each time I meet her, I learn more from her than she learns from me." He says the young woman, Diane Kastama, was paralyzed from the waist down in a car accident. He finds it impressive that, along with competing, she breeds appaloosas and works forty hours per week in the computer industry. Zantke says he has high hopes for her, and for the two other disabled team members who represent the U.S. in international competitions. In 2002, they brought home a team Bronze and an Individual Silver Medal.

Hardy and Jutta Zantke work with their own horses at Rolling Hills Estates, an equestrian community near Torrance. Jutta trains young horses under saddle, using the principles of dressage.

Zantke has not participate in world championship events as a driver, but he holds nearly all important first-place titles in the western United States in both pairs and four-in-hand. "This has been my hobby," he says, adding that he is not sure how far he wants to go in competition. Zantke says that aging is somewhat of a disadvantage in competition because the sport requires excellent memory and quick reflexes. "Ultimately, you have too much experience," he says. "The young guys go for broke – they either crash or they win. When you're older, you don't risk as much." Zantke says there are exceptions to that rule, however, and that several top European drivers are not young. Although he enjoys competition, he finds great satisfaction in the other ways he is presently involved in the sport.

Zantke's enthusiasm for Combined Driving has helped to build the sport in America. He admits that participation is expensive, but he believes there is opportunity for success for anyone who is truly committed. "If you want it badly enough, and if you are good enough, you can do it – from any background," he says with characteristic optimism. "If you dedicate your life to it, you can do it. I'm sure."

Kentucky Horse Park,
Lexington, Kentucy

The Legacy
of the
Carriage Horse

Gloria Austin AND THE *Austin Carriage Museum*

Before the advent of the automobile, horses and carriages met the needs of everyday transportation in Europe and America, and wealthier citizens traveled in fine carriages pulled by exquisitely matched pairs or teams. Today, hundreds of carriage drivers in the United States and Europe still practice the discipline, both for pleasure and in the show ring.

Gloria Austin, founder of the Austin Carriage Museum, holds many championship titles in Carriage Driving, including American Four-In-Hand Pleasure Driving and Coaching Champion. She has been a devoted promoter and patron of Carriage Driving for the past two decades. The Austin Carriage Museum is located at Continental Acres Equine Resort in Weirsdale, Florida, which Austin owns and operates. She is also the founder of the Gloria Austin Foundation, Inc., a nonprofit foundation that operates the museum and the Austin Education Center. The foundation promotes educational, cultural-historical, and scientific activities devoted to the horse and carriage.

Austin, who grew up in rural, upstate New York, says she became interested in horses while watching Roy Rogers, Dale Evans, Gene Autry, and the Cisco

Sunday morning at Walnut Hill Competition, New York

Kid on Saturday morning television as a child. Her father operated a dairy farm and also loved horses, so she says it was not difficult to convince him to buy her a horse. His first job had been driving a team of draft horses on road construction. Austin says he would load her horse into his cattle truck and drive her to local club shows, and in return, she promised to gather cows with her horse when needed.

When Austin was twenty, she sold her saddle horse for college books, and was without a horse for twenty years. At age forty, she felt she could afford to maintain and devote time to a horse once more. Austin purchased a registered Paint horse and rode it in the hills of northwestern New Jersey. "I was working in northern New Jersey and New York City at the time," she says, "and my horse was a refuge from the hustle and bustle of a fast-paced lifestyle."

Unicorn Team at the Walnut Hill Competition

When she moved to upstate New York, she began to have trouble with her knees when she returned to riding each spring. "One spring I had to wrap one knee, and the next spring I had to wrap both," she says, "so I decided I needed to look for another way to enjoy the horses." She attended the Royal Winter Agricultural Fair in Toronto, Canada, and knew she had found a solution. "I saw what looked to be very old, frail gentlemen driving four horses to magnificent coaches." As she watched, Austin was sure it was something she could do. She says she immediately purchased a trained Welsh-Arab pony, as well as a runabout carriage and a sleigh.

After driving the pony, Austin purchased a Palomino Quarter Horse. Next, she bought a pair of Morgans, and then a single Saddlebred. As her involvement with Carriage Driving grew, she added more horses. She purchased a pair of Morgan-Friesian crossbreeds, a four-in-hand of Friesians, and a four-in-hand of Kladruby horses from the Czech Republic.

Although it is easy to understand the nostalgic charm of an antique

Cross Country Course at the Walnut Hill Competition

carriage pulled by four beautiful horses, Austin says most people don't comprehend the excitement of Carriage Driving. "You are driving four horses that each weigh 1,500 pounds, plus the carriage," she says. "With one hand, you are controlling five tons. If that doesn't give you a thrill – to drive that up and down the roadways or in the show ring – I don't know what will."

Austin's career was greatly influenced by the Walnut Hill Driving Competition, which has been held annually since 1970. "The ambiance of this show led me to improve the quality of my turnouts," she says. Austin is on the board of directors, and has competed in the show for more than fifteen years. She says the show stresses the importance of driving restored antique carriages in the traditional style. It is the largest competition of its kind, and boasts more than two hundred entrants. The event has its roots in a group of carriage drivers that once gathered on Sundays to enjoy driving their carriages and to have picnics with other drivers. Austin says the tradition survives, and in order to win championships, competitors must participate in the Sunday pleasure drive.

She began collecting single-horse carriages when she drove a single horse,

The Water Crossing at Walnut Hill Competition

then began buying pair carriages and, eventually, progressed to four-in-hand. Austin bought her first collectible, a wicker carriage with a parasol top, at an auction in Pennsylvania. She continued to collect antique harnesses and vehicles, and her collection now includes more than 170 carriages. In 2000, Austin opened the Austin Carriage Museum, nestled in the center of the 365-acre Continental Acres Equine Resort in the northern part of Lake County, Florida. Most of the carriages displayed at the museum have been fully restored to their original splendor. Many are brightly painted and lavishly upholstered in tufted silk and leather, with gleaming brass ornaments and working lamps.

The carriage styles range from functional to flamboyant. The collection includes a French muletaire from the 1700s and a reindeer sleigh from the same era. Also displayed is a gala coupe once owned by Emperor Franz-Joseph, which is embellished with gold-leaf décor, has gold-plated lamps, and gold threads woven into the hammercloth. More common carriages are also featured, including a stagecoach, a chuckwagon, a medicine carriage, a U.S. mail cart, and a large hunting carriage with a dog compartment.

"We use each carriage in the museum to tell a story about a lifestyle that no longer exists," Austin says. "The East Gallery tells the story of the European aristocrats, and the West Gallery tells the American story." Two early cars are included in the collection to show the influence carriages had on automobiles, and to explain what happened to carriage manufacturers once cars were invented. "I like to tell people that we have had over 5,000 years of history with the horse as our means of transportation, and only one hundred years with self-propelled transportation," Austin explains. "We are here to tell of those 5,000 years when the horse provided us with food, aided us in war, took us from place to place, provided us with much pleasure, and had a tremendous impact on history. Sadly, the story of the role of the horse and the carriage are never told."

Austin says that although early Americans liked to emulate the European gentry who traveled in fine carriages with matched teams, they lacked the financial resources. The earliest American carriages were often lightweight and were made for a single horse. One resource that was available to Americans was wood, and Austin says as many as five types were sometimes used to build one carriage. A system of roads and bridges developed in concert with carriages, and Austin says the width of both railroad tracks and automobiles parallels the width of the

popular carriage. New England towns, she says, are spaced eight to ten miles apart because a horse could sustain an 8-10 mile per hour trot comfortably for about an hour.

The Golden Age of the carriage, says Austin, was the late 1800s when the industrial revolution made possible the production of affordable, well-made carriages. American manufacturers each added unique design features, and some, such as Studebaker, made the transition to automobile manufacturing. The Concord line, which included the American Western stagecoach, had ceased production by the end of the nineteenth century.

An early institution in America was the Sunday pleasure drive. "Families hitched their best horse to their best carriage, dressed in their best clothes, and drove to the park for a picnic, visited Aunt Sarah, or went to a race meet or polo match," Austin says. "Then, they unhitched the horses and used the carriage as a grandstand." She says speed limits were enforced on roadways. Although they couldn't be measured, the rule was that one horse must be at a trot.

The resort that houses the museum and educational center was established for people who want to vacation with or train their horses in sunny Florida, where horses can be enjoyed year-round. Ninety-one stalls in eight barns are located throughout the property, which is adorned with graceful live oaks draped with Spanish Moss, and features two lakes. Guests also have access to dressage rings, a round pen, hazards, cones, and wooded, winding trails that lace the property.

Four of Austin's twenty-seven Carriage Driving horses are stabled in Europe where she travels in May, July and September to compete in traditional Driving events. She keeps these horses and a number of restored antique carriages in Belgium, so they are available for private drives and competitions in Great Britain, France, Belgium, Holland and Germany.

In Carriage Driving competitions, Austin says grooms dress in traditional costumes while passengers and drivers wear conservative contemporary attire. In some competitions, passengers and grooms are required. Scores are dependent upon a beautiful turnout. Austin says it is one of the few competitive events where men and women are evenly matched. The horse, she says, is the great equalizer.

Austin lives at Continental Acres Equine Resort with her husband, Vernon Eddy. She has a daughter, six grandchildren, and a handicapped son who live in New York state. She is a trustee with the B. Thomas Golisano Foundation, and through personal gifts, Austin is involved in services to the handicapped. She is also on the Board of Directors of the Carriage Association of America. Gloria Austin's dedication to preserving the legacy of Carriage Driving enables others to enjoy the rich heritage of the horse, which has served mankind in battle, in commerce, and in sport for more than four millennia.